HOW BUSINESS FAILS US
What You Need To Know
About Business Corruption

I0464284

© Copyright Kip Koehler 2012-15
kipkoehler.com

Table Of Contents

What Were They Thinkin'?

Power is not inherently evil, or is it? Ordinary people who have great power visited upon them through their efforts or happy convenience may become changed for the worse. They are no longer ordinary to themselves. Their inner voice tells them that the rules which other have to live by no longer apply, if breaking them is done with stealth. The devil on one shoulder speaks to them more forcefully than the angel on the other.

People in positions of power may revert to their childhood behavior of wanting to have all of the toys, to the point where they will do virtually anything to get them. Having <u>some</u> is never quite as fulfilling as having <u>more</u>. Multiple, expensive objects can be the objective of an intense desire, and the examples of this behavior are too numerous to mention. This need, far too often, leads to unethical, immoral, or criminal activities in their business dealings. One might think that the number of these miscreants that end up being exposed or land in jail would act as a deterrent to others with insatiable desires. But that appears not to be the case. Apparently great power, like some drugs, dulls the wit.

Fleecing the public should not have to remain a secret for long if we are paying attention to overt manifestations of wealth. One possible conclusion about this lack of exposure is that others who are also at the top of this game are playing in the same ballpark. Perhaps they are keeping their own secrets and respecting those of their peers. Rats do not rat in other rats.

Voting for any candidate is an essentially a futile exercise, and it denies the truth of corporate manipulation, regardless of which party is elected.

They Auto Do Better

What may be one of the more pathetic businesses in America has been the auto industry. At one time there were a half dozen thriving manufacturers, and that is now down to three. They have gone from producing virtually all US vehicles to producing only a fraction of them. In 2011 GM and Ford's share of the market was less than 20% each.

It's not as if this sorry condition beset the industry overnight. The downhill slide took some fifty years of arrogance to accomplish. That means fifty years of not minding the store while the executives were drawing fancy salaries and bonuses.

How did the industry let this tragedy occur? There are several factors that took place over time...
-- several smaller *(that are now out of business)* manufacturers thought that they could get away with building poor quality cars just because the Big Three did
-- when times were good and there was not yet competition from Japan, the manufacturers gave away massive future profits to the unions by granting excessive benefits packages, on top of good salaries
-- the sales model for Detroit was to build bigger clunkers, even while automobile demand was inexorably changing toward higher quality and greater fuel efficiency
-- billions of advertising dollars were spent *(wasted)* on marketing to the diminishing number of Americans who still believed in Detroit's *bigger is better* line of thinking
-- lobbying congress to keep the automobile mileage requirements in check in order to permit the greater profit margins on the sale of their oversized slugs
-- ignoring the flood of high quality, imported cars until it was too late to mount an effective counterattack, and it may be too late *(short of some miracle)* for Detroit to convince us that they do know what is expected and will perform accordingly

Prior to a modest recovery, the government had an opportunity to provide a long term solution to Detroit's financial problems by...
-- temporarily taking over the auto companies with bailout funds and debt repayment provisions
-- firing the incompetent top executives and boards of directors
-- replacing these people with executives who have demonstrated an ability to manage corporations efficiently
-- forcing the unions to make reasonable concessions to limit the blood loss

-- insisting on building quality cars that will compete effectively with those coming from abroad

Dumbthink is of course not restricted to automobile companies. In what may be one of the lamest decisions by corporate America, Pfizer Inc. decided to commit more than $87 million toward promoting their previous cash cow, Lipitor. Now this may not seem too outrageous in the high finance world of the drug empire, but this judgment was made after their patent had expired in the fall of 2011. I guess they thought that they could become the Kleenex of this particular segment of prescription drugs. With generic replacements coming onto the market in the future, this was a risky call.

Airline Cattle Call

Let me suggest what might have been a dicey decision adopted by the airline industry… the Airbus 380. You know, that huge double decked aircraft that can tote a megaton of people and their luggage half way across the world without having to refuel. Apparently the developers and the purchasing airlines felt a pressing need for their airplanes to live up to the name <u>bus</u>. It surely can't be that people want to embark/debark a plane with several hundred more people than now, and have even more lost bags.

Talk about catering to the bottom line rather than to the comfort and convenience of the passengers. But this is the direction that our air carriers have been taking for years as they gobbled each other up. They have made air travel anathema to most of us… an experience to avoid whenever possible. When my wife and I used to fly to of San Francisco *(which is some twelve hours away by car)* we experienced the…
-- transit times to and from the airport
-- security screening
-- waiting for the plane to be given a gate
-- waiting for boarding to begin
-- waiting for the plane to fill
-- waiting for takeoff clearance
-- the length of the flight, of course
-- waiting at baggage pick up
-- taking ground transportation to a hotel

-- other holdups

With all of these delays, air travel to SF can take about the same amount of time as it does by car. So why fly and then have to suffer the additional expense and delay of renting a car? Even with the price of gas, the cost of driving is still less than air fare for two. And it immensely more enjoyable if one has the endurance for long distance car travel with occasional stops.

No Class First Class

It has been some time since first class travel on the US airlines has resembled its previous level of comfort and attention. While the seats are about the same, catering to the passengers has fallen off sharply.

On an early evening flight last year our US Airways' first class meal consisted of multiple bagged snacks and free drinks. This was, however, more than the single bag that was offered to the economy seat patrons. Wow. The stated justification for this lack of service, according to the attendant, was that it was past <u>their</u> dinner hour. Sorry, but it was <u>our</u> dinner hour. And of course the airline did not take into consideration that people may be traveling without food to the airport, and then waiting to board during <u>their</u> dinner hour.

In 2012 the airlines had decided to reduce the number of first class seats because 75 percent of them are occupied by mileage-point passengers or by those who upgrade to first class using points. That is a non-revenue scenario that hurts the bottom line, and which leaves the carriers with a limited incentive to provide this comfort. It also leaves people with additional, unspent mileage points.

Forget that the airlines doled out or had sold points for flying in their planes or using their credit cards. Their contracts to provide seats to is mostly hot air unless you are willing to fly at off-peak times, on circuitous routes, or manage to book one or two of the few seats that they allocate to points passengers on a seemingly random basis. Of course you can usually get a seat if you cough up two or more times the normal number of points. And this outrage must be well known to the government which does nothing to rein in what I consider a fraud on the public.

And while I'm on the flying topic, what is with the 250-300 pounders who think they can sit in coach seats and overflow fat into their neighbor's space. Just as annoying, besides crying babies, are those who fly in social clusters and think that the fuselage is their private partying room, regardless of the hour. Flying has truly become an unpleasant cattle car experience.

Personal Competition

If you are a Creationist you may not have relevant arguments about the nature and derivation of the behaviors that are exhibited by modern people because we were all created at the same time as our bacteria. But if you examine evolution, it can be useful to give meaning to our social and anti-social traits. The behaviors that we have developed conspire to make us what we are today, like it or not.

One of these negative traits involves competitive behavior. This is an attribute which would normally be deemed to be a positive trait, but can occasionally be something else. Whether it is when we are participating in sports, business, or mate selection, some degree of competition is a given, and it is usually constructive.

But competition did not materialize out of thin air or by the grace of God. It became hard-wired into our brains during the search for and the retention of mates, food and security. Those who were most adept at finding and protecting their resources influenced the rest of us by having those beneficial behaviors passed on to successive generations via their genes. If there was no success, there were no successive generations. It could not be more straightforward.

So competition is a genetic imperative that has been handed down to us even though we have moved further away from the difficulties that led to its development. Today we continue to view these behaviors as being as asset, and will sometimes overlook their adverse side effects because of our conditioning. For example, what could be more unacceptable than...
-- dog or cock fights
-- drinking contests
-- bar altercations

-- road rage
-- professional boxing
-- phony wrestling
-- assault hockey
-- basketball as a contact sport
-- the escalating number of fights in the sports arenas

So it appears that not all competition is productive. The negative side of this activity can also be observed in the widespread and lightly reported use of illegal drugs in virtually all sports. Since for some winning is not everything, it is the only thing, cheating is a big part of that only thing.

Business Competition

Competition rightfully exists in business, but the fight for consumer dollars can lead to amoral, unethical behaviors in that undertaking such as…
-- making secret, anticompetitive deals with other companies
-- the solicitation of insider information
-- business espionage
-- concealing cost saving from alterations to a product's formula

This last item is common way to make a buck by deceiving the public when it is accomplished by reformulating a recipe so that it…
-- may appear to have been improved
-- can legally be claimed to be 'new and improved'
-- uses fewer and less expensive ingredients without a corresponding reduction in price

Every now and then a company announces that a product contains a 10% (or whatever) increase in some valued ingredient. More than when exactly? Did they also reduce that particular ingredient over the last months or years only to then be able to tout a contrived improvement? The answer to this question is occasionally yes. How many time over the years have we heard that the same candy bar now has 10% more chocolate? If this were true, with out incremental reductions, the bar's weight might a pound by now.

The food industry commonly reduces the amount of an ingredient in a product when wholesale costs escalate… all without informing the public of any change to the product, unless they use the phony new and improved claim *(a quality that may rest in the pen of the creative since the feds make no effort to verify it).* This lack of meaningful disclosure of a change in ingredients is simple deceit, and has been businesses way of doing business for years.

Since corporate non-disclosure occurs with some regularity, one can assume that my negative interpretation of business practices has validity. It would be helpful to see a regulation put in place that would require companies to reveal when an adjustment to a formula has taken place that significantly alters a product. If their recipes are proprietary for valid reasons, they should not have to disclose the exact alterations, but a mandatory notification of some sort might alert the public to any unconstructive change.

Years ago a chocolate drink powder was introduced using a puffed-up formulation which permitted quicker mixing with milk. Since the objective of the new chemistry was not done to con the public, the puffed-up mix came in a rather large jar at a smaller jar's price. Once its success in the marketplace was recognized, the chemistry was adopted in a preexisting drink mix. Within a short time, the original product was dropped from the store shelves and the newly-puffed product was packaged in its original, smaller jar for about the same price as its previous non-puffed powder. So instead of using two tablespoons to make a glass of chocolate milk, it took three or more… a significant increase to the consumer and profit to the manufacturer.

Eventually the manufacturer returned to what appears to be the original formula packaged in what looks to be the original jar's container size. Apparently there is <u>not</u> a sucker born every minute as they expected. Consumer price resistance was probably a factor in this turn about. Score one for the good guys.

In a similar fashion to the chocolate powder caper above, we should be aware of the puffing of ice cream to the point where in most cases it is essentially frozen air… no exaggeration, more air *(sometimes 60% more)* than liquid. This weight reduction practice started more than fifty years ago and has continued unabated ever since, with just a few notable exceptions in the super-premium *(real ice cream)* sector.

With regular ice cream, chemicals such as edible glue have replaced cream as the primary thickener rather than butterfat. And law makers have permitted this reduction in quality to exist without intervention.

FYI - Did you know that low fat ice cream usually contains more sweetener and calories than regular ice cream in order to offset the less desirable taste of what should no longer be labeled ice cream?

We can thank the efforts of the dairy industry for getting legislators to support their deliberate program of putting less and less of a product in the same size container. Because ice cream is sold by volume, not weight, replacing the solid portion of the ice cream with air does not require a reduction in the container size. Over the years, efforts by consumer advocates have failed to get ice cream sold by its weight *(as it rightly should be)* due to industry lobbying *(bribery)*.

Can you imagine a can of peaches sold with more juice than fruit and the manufacturer getting away with it? Well if that wasn't enough of an industry assault on a staple, the half-gallon *(2 qt)* cartons have been volume-adjusted downward to the current 1.5 quart standard in stages to help obfuscate the change. Apparently the manufactures shamefully figure that the public does not pay attention to product sizing, and they are not far wrong.

If one looks around with a critical eye it is possible to see similar actions being taken industry wide across a broad spectrum of products, and to what good end? When virtually all companies conform to a new, smaller size, or they similarly convert their product to less costly ingredients, they are all in the same boat, competitively speaking. What the chemical industry *(who may be the biggest benefactor)* supplies to one manufacturer, they can supply to all.

Logic might indicate that this sizing and ingredient modification behavior is actually a stimulating, competitive game, and that businesses enjoy it just for the fun it provides. It certainly can't be that they get off on retooling their production lines from time to time, for no long term advantage. What ever happened to the effort to get all products delivered in standard sizes or weights anyway?

On the other hand, what resizing, reformulating, and other dodges do is to pump up the *potential* profit margin so that the corporations can indulge in the all-to-common practice of running the discounts that are so attractive to consumers. In industry-speak it is called *high/lo pricing*. To put it another way, companies end up with bloated margins in order to have impressive sales price reductions on some sort of predetermined schedule. But with competition being wide spread among manufacturers, everyone is basically on a level playing field, and no one gains any lasting advantage.

The big winners may be the newspapers who get to broadcast the weekly sales with their multi-page ads. The losers are those who receive inferior products or end up paying higher prices in order to support the advertising cost of those recurring discounts.

FYI - When a chef from the Food Channel was asked which olive oil she purchased, her response was "The one that's on sale - one is always on sale". You might do the same for the products you buy.

I suppose there may be a slight advantage to having bloated list prices among those shoppers who are more impressed with their savings than they are with their expenditures. Wouldn't you think that they might get a clue when there are frequent clothing sales of 70% off or more? Do they think that these businesses are in the money losing trade?

Peripheral issues to contrived sales are the grocery and cosmetic coupons that are touted by newspaper and Internet sites. Essentially these are offers to induce customers to buy things that they may not need or want. I am amused when a housewife is shown saving $100 or more with her shopping cart full of items. Virtually all of those grocery coupons are for junk food and not for healthy, fresh, or fresh frozen foods.

Going back to sizing. When I was a kid the large potato chip box was 16 ounces in weight from virtually every vendor. Gradually, so that few might take notice, the size of the inner bag in the box was reduced ounce by ounce. Eventually when the smaller bags looked silly in the box and became too small in size to be convenient for the homemaker, a colossal, new 1 pound box was introduced. This downsizing and upsizing has happened many times over the years because so few pay attention to, or object to the manipulation of the consumer.

At one time the 14.5 ounce can of vegetables was 16 ounces. And why is it 14.5 ounces anyway? Well do the math. Actually doing the math is the problem because this odd sizing game makes price comparisons more difficult. The conversions to obtuse sizing have become so flagrant that grocery stores may include a cost-per-ounce or similar listings on their shelf labels for those with the inclination to use them. Do we need more proof than this that manufactures are working to obfuscate their pricing to the public?

Then there is the cosmetic industry. This is a large group of companies that have taken prevarication to new lows. Recently it was the essence of avocado that did wonders. Before that is was milk and botanicals. Then it was mushrooms. Oh no, not any ordinary mushrooms, but Portobello mushrooms… presumably because they are known to be a gourmet treat. We can only hope that it will not be garlic's or cabbages' turn next.

Business Rip Offs

In 2010 it was reported that several insurance companies had taken advantage of the relatives of deceased soldiers. They managed the death benefits, earned some 5% on these accounts, and then paid out about 1% in interest to the relatives. The retained difference amounted to healthy windfall for this handful of companies. A class action suit was eventually initiated to recover these ill-gotten gains. This again shows how big business can be corrupted by its quest for ever greater profits.

In 2012 a superstorm named Sandy smashed into the East Coast of the US. Flood insurance companies, working with FEMA, sent an army of engineers to investigate its damage. Their assigned task was to discover how much of the devastation to policy holder's homes was caused by the surging seawater and how much of it predated the storm.

More than two years later a group of lawyers that are representing about 1500 homeowners are attempting to prove that a number of the engineering firms that were hired to inspect the damage issued false reports in order to give insurers sufficient justification to deny claims. For example, some broken home foundations were allegedly blamed on poor construction or on settling of the soil. In other cases cracked or warped walls were being attributed to the building's old age. As of 2015 the verdict is not yet in.

The home/small-office printer and ink cartridge business is an excellent case of an all-too-clever business plan with their: *set prices low now, get large profits in the future scheme...* one that we should all be aware of. There are also many other companies that function in this devious way. The game is to price the non-disposable part of a product near or below the cost of manufacture to encourage sales, then make up for the tiny profit or initial loss with the highly profitable, disposable items that are used by these products. Printers and ink cartridges are a part of this notorious business plan. In a few cases these printers have actually priced below the cost of replacement printer cartridges. In one particular case that I noted, a new printer was priced at about 30 percent less that its cartridges.

For my printing needs I have chosen to purchase cartridges from a third party supplier at a discount. The potential downside to this method of replacement can be the loss of warranty *(who cares)* and the products may shorten a printer's lifespan *(not likely)*. I have experienced a few faulty cartridges that were replaced for free, but have not yet had a printer issue.

In 2013 Anheuser-Busch was accused, in a $5 million, false-labeling, class-action lawsuit, of watering down its beer. Their labels state 5% as the alcohol content for the regular beer, while some light versions are said to be 4+%. However, it is alleged that the alcohol content has been reduced by 3 to 8 percent with the addition of water to the batches after normal brewing. Since the manufacturing tax fees vary based on the amount of alcohol in a product, I wonder if A-B notified the government of the change to reduce their taxes. It is likely they were just content having to brew less alcohol for their dollar intake.

Absence of Standards

As a beginning programmer I was expected to learn the coding standards for software so that the end-user would not be required to guess or research what to do next when running my program. For the most part, our community has generally improved somewhat on these techniques over the years. As a result, software usually functions in a similar, reasonable way from program to program. When using a program, if I am required to read the instructions before running the software, I know that the programmer or analyst had not done their job well.

Other industries are another matter. Perhaps the most glaring absence of standards is with the electronics industry's remote control units, whether for the DVD player, surround sound, or the TV itself. Those who are employed to design these devices apparently lock themselves in window-less, phone-less, rooms without meaningful contact with the outside world, except during bathroom breaks. The result is what one might expect. There is little rhyme or reason to the button layouts from one manufacturer to the next. And remotes do not function with other manufacturer's products. And why not? There is no reasonable answer to that query.

What must surely be the worst case of remotes-out-of-control are the TV/DVD controllers which can be found in hotels and resorts. Even with my background in electronics, using these devices is anything but simple. I imagine that the hotel's engineers are driven crazy having to repeatedly explain the functions and missing functions to the guests.

To a lesser degree, the automobile industry functions in a similar mode. Driving a different car should not mean having to retrieve the operating manual or suffer minutes of concentration before one embarks. Yet being an occasional rental customer I know this expectation is a flight of fancy. Try to figure out how to manipulate the windshield wiper control for a very light rain sometime.

It's not as if having product designers who are trained to observe the consensus of standards were an insurmountable process. It just requires a little communication and compromise with others in the same industry. But companies behave like the political parties do... the other guys are their mortal enemies. It's a worse than silly position, and like politics, their attitudes makes it our loss.

Another absence of standards revolves around the way in which items are rated. Years back a problem surfaced when companies were stating their size of computer video displays. Eventually a universal, diagonal measurement was settled on after disgruntled consumers played the lawyer card.

Today, flat screen television sets and monitors are another example of a standards issue. One of the common measurements of quality resides in the contrast ratio *(the difference between pure black and pure white)*, but not all manufactures use the same testing algorithm *(mathematical formula)* to calculate this measurement. One company's stated ratio of 25.000 to 1 may be better than another company's ratio of 50.000 to 1. And it is not as if the one with the deceptive rating does not know what they are doing. But because the government does not oversee this process, the manufacturers feel free to fudge the numbers without fear of retribution... again, until someone plays the lawyer card.

Excessive Promotion

If I were to identify the one business that is the most corrupt from a consumer aspect it would be the cosmetics industry. Virtually nothing that they tout to be miracle skin rejuvenation products is even modestly effective, but this does nothing to stop new remedies from regularly being added to their advertising budgets. When the initial flood of purchases dies off and they become uneconomical to promote, it's on to the next name in this name-game scenario.

Every now and then one of these companies *(usually of modest size)* develops an aggressive business plan that is intended to take it into the big leagues. A few years back a cosmetics company created its variety of products for consumers. Then they went on a spending binge with an immense advertising budget and unsubstantiated claims to capture a share of this large segment. A research article indicated that this company was spending 85% of its income on advertising and only 15% on their products, company administration, and debt. Based on how little they allocated to R&D it's likely that their products consisted of easily purchased ingredients and did not represent cutting edge anything. The advertising blitz went on for a few years, and then just as quickly as they came on the scene they dropped off of the map, probably when too many consumers discovered that their wares did not live up to the hype.

In 2014 members of the automobile insurance industry had begun engaging in this same breakout tactic… massive, dishonest ads to obtain a bigger slice of a large pie. Since huge budgets are being directed into these campaigns, how much can be left over for filling auto claims fairly, or for the unbelievable rate savings that are claimed. And how can they all be cheaper than the others?

Deceitful Promotion

The propaganda surrounding product advertising has for some time been used to promote their industries as being beneficial to the consumer. It alleges to introduce us to new products and exposes us to what we might need to know. Without advertising, so the story goes, many good ideas might languish in the minds of their creators and not become known to the public.

Unfortunately the bad comes hand in hand with the alleged good. This is because there is only minimal government intervention into the deceptive practices of business. Corporations are free to extol the nonexistent virtues that they assign to their products without fear of contradiction or retribution. In some cases this deception takes the form of its packaging graphics. That is, the paper and ink package presentation of a product may have little connection to the contents that are inside.

Some foods use manicured *"serving suggestion"* pictures on the outside of the box, or they may offer the equally deceptive *"enlarged to show detail"* statement in their ads. How these images relate to what is on the inside a package or what the actual sizing of an item is must reside in a purchaser's imagination.

In a similar vein some years ago, a major soup manufacturer was discovered putting clear marbles in bottom of its televised soup bowls so that the solid ingredients would sit near the surface and look more substantial. And what was the punishment for this unrealistic display? It was a cease and desist order. That's all. Not exactly a stinging rebuke that might deter the next company from perpetrating such a fraud.

Also years ago the milk industry came up with a slogan for an ad campaign that promoted milk as *"Natures most nearly perfect food"*. This advertising ran for months before the misstatement of fact was forced off of the airwaves. Later they were back with the catchy phrase of *"Good for every body"*, and again they were required to retract their ads. More recently, milk had been promoted as having a beneficial effect on dieting. And again they were required to delete these commercials because of having no evidence to support their dubious contention. They just don't give up, do they?

These ongoing efforts by industries don't surprise me because there is virtually no economic downside to these calculated misstatements of fact. Their message can be removed from circulation, but the public may remember it and never realize that it was nothing more than a clever marketing phrase with no scientific support, and that the misstatement of fact had been forced off of the airwaves.

So the FDA issues their directive, and that is the end of it. No public rebuke, rarely an order for corrective advertising, generally no fines or other penalties, just a brief interruption in corrupt business-as-usual.

One extremely rare exception to the slap on the wrist was a juice packager that made misleading claims about their products. They were subsequently required to purchase a substantial amount corrective advertising. So what did they do? Did they have to explain that they had lied? No. They were permitted to advertise that their juice had a certain, small percent of real fruit juice as if that was an advantage to the consumer. After a run of these corrective ads and a loss of consumer interest, this particular item dropped off the map. Maybe the public can see, just don't hold your breath.

Excessive and fraudulent commercials are more evidence of how the government is run by big business.

A government/business promotion that dwarfed much of industries advertising was the elevation of corn to rock star status in the search for sustainable energy sources. Yes...
-- like other grains it can produce ethanol
-- we still have some suitable land left that can be used for additional corn production
-- we do need alternative sources of fuel if we are not going to reduce our dependence on foreign energy
-- it would benefit some farmers *(especially the already prosperous agribusiness farms with millions of planted acres)*

But what almost no one tells us is that...
-- ethanol has a 30% less energy content than gasoline *(to be fair, ethanol is 113 octane, and if cars were specifically tuned for this with a higher compression ratio and more substantial plumbing, the energy output would become equivalent, but that has not happened)*
-- the energy in a gallon of ethanol is only marginally more than the energy that is needed to produce it *(a study by Cornell University stated that it takes 1.3 gallons of oil to produce 1 gallon of ethanol when every aspect of production and delivery is considered)*
-- the price of corn, corn products, and corn fed for livestock has escalated as corn's new demand moved it from corn-the-food-crop toward corn-the-energy-crop
-- the agribusiness corn producers are the big winners
-- politicians benefit from the massive amounts of money that are diverted from the loose pockets of agribusiness
-- demand for oil and all of the ills that accompany it goes on virtually unabated

If the above is not convincing enough, consider that a full sized SUV requires 450 pounds of corn in order to yield enough ethanol to fill its tank. That is 450 pounds of a crop that can not be of benefit to us elsewhere, including foreign exchange. And this use of corn has driven up the prices of feed animals and the consumer products that rely on corn. Some proof of this is that in the fall of 2011 the price of corn had risen 16 percent over the previous year. Have you noticed beef prices lately?

Deceitful Representation

From fast food to frozen food, figures don't lie, but liars sure can figure. According to news reports these industries are well known for underrating the calorie counts of their products by as much as 30%. The government may require posting this information on a label or a wall, but apparently they have no inclination to verify the results. Perhaps they figure a close call is sufficient for consumers to make informed judgments. Or more likely it is that they assume their going through the motions of industry oversight will keep us off of their backs. Also, does lobbying come to mind?

What could be more dishonest than the blizzard of phony claims and intentionally misleading statements that are made on a daily basis by the food, cosmetic, and other industries? Quasi-terms and labels are invented to sound meaningful but may have no basis in English or in any facts that they might imply.

Perhaps the most abused word is *natural*. There is no legal definition to this word, but it is freely used to impart the illusion of goodness to many products. Have you ever bought a natural hair spray? What exactly could be natural about hair spray? Is there a hair spray plant somewhere that I don't know about?

Virtually every ad on television is laced with some degree of sounds-impressive-but-says-nothing verbiage to deceive and manipulate consumers. A buyer's judgment should be that if it sounds too good it is probably a prevarication.

Mark Twain: *"Get your facts first, and then you can distort em as much as you please."*

As one example among many, a cosmetics company uses a coined word in their advertising that is similar to regenerate. According the dictionary their word means... oops, the word is not in the dictionary. It was created for the illusionary effect that it could produce in the mind of the consumer. A product with regenerative qualities must surely accomplish something, right?

A number of companies use this faux-word technique because of the gullibility of consumers and the recognition of this by the advertisers. In recent years there have been a number of new ice-cream-like names that are used for what we might assume to be real ice cream, but are not. If you *churn* something, isn't it ice cream? These invented, cutie, names are used so that the label does not have to disclose something like: *this product does not even come close to being real ice cream.*

An often-abused word is *fresh*. It may or may not mean what you think it does, and this term reaches the zenith of obfuscation with the term *fresh frozen*. So is it fresh or is it frozen? Is it frozen while fresh as apposed to being frozen after rotting? Many of us will recognize the dichotomy of juxtaposing these two words, but this does nothing to prevent food companies from utilizing advertising doublespeak to influence those who are easily misled.

Another highly deceptive use of words is to describe a product using the term made <u>with</u>. This widespread and misleading phraseology works to a manufacturer's advantage because the average person will assume they are being told that a product is basically made <u>of</u> some ingredient or material, when in fact they are being told no such thing. <u>Made of</u> means composed of a single ingredient. <u>Made with</u> carries no such denotation. It only means that it contains <u>some</u> of an ingredient.

One restaurant chain claimed that their burgers were made with three, desirable, cuts of prime beef. And of course they do not say how much of each is used. Is it 3% or 33%? We don't actually know because the intention of the ad was meant to mislead, not inform. These folks rightfully figure that people may assume that there is some sort of even ingredients split in the burgers. The ad further suggests that their burgers taste better than those that are made from other *(and perhaps just as tasty)* cuts. That is another non-justified statement that is also meant to impress but not inform.

Then there is the breakfast syrup that is no longer made with any butter as its name implies. When it first came out it specified having 2% butter on its ingredients list. Now that the consumers may have become aware of its butter content and taste, that component has been reduced to 0%. So did the manufacturer disclose this significant change, other than its absence from the ingredients list? Did they remove the word butter from the name? Nope. Instead it now claims that the product is *buttery*, in its ads. So apparently a claim of being buttery and not actually containing any butter is ok with the manufacturer and the feds, even if it may not be ok with the rest of us.

One of the pet food purveyors claims that their dog food "Does not contain any <u>added</u> hormones". Would this surprise anyone? Do companies buy hormones by the bucket so that they can add it to their prepared food? Aren't hormones given to feed animals to increase their growth potential? Please note that the company in question did not claim that their food did <u>not</u> contain any hormones. They also stated that their pet food does not contain any <u>added</u> antibiotics. Same story here.

Many of the products that we buy have a similar, cavalier, attitude toward the dispensing the truth. Misleading the public, it seems, is not against the law, as witnessed by the fact that there are so many corporations indulging in this practice. And it gives the 'creatives' something to do for a living.

Another product has also succumbed to the shrink the size rather than raise the price strategy. I picked up a quart of mayonnaise at the grocery and discovered that their standard jars are now only 15 and 30 ounces in size. Can 13 and 26 ounces be far away?

On the soft drink front, a small soda carrier holds 6 bottles or cans of the beverage. The next size up holds double that, or 12 bottles or cans as we might expect. With this established progression in mind, one would not be blamed for assuming that the next larger packaging size would contain 24. Nope! It holds only 20... 4 short of doubling the previous size. At first glance the large case might even look like it holds 24 containers with its long, thin, *(purposely deceiving?)* design. This is probably what the vendors would like you to think when you try to compute its cost per bottle or can. Let's see... if 12 sodas cost $4.95 and 20 cost $8.49, quick - which is the better value?

An area that seems to be on the increase is store brand pricing. While most of us would expect this to be an area where bargains can be found, it may not always be the case. Apparently the chain stores are finding this to be a nice profit center for them. In addition there may be some deception involved in the packaging. I noticed that one stores pasta boxes were the same size as a popular brand, but the contents were 12 ounces, not the normal 16 ounces, making the cost per ounce higher for the store's product during the frequent sales of the name brand box.

An article in a scientific magazine alleged that the holistic or health formula industry had virtually no products that were, or could be proven to be either safe or effective. But you wouldn't know this from looking at the health-store shelves that are packed with 'cures and remedies'. And do the consumers of these products really know anything about them that does not come from highly unreliable word of mouth of clerks and some users?

Because these formulas are not drugs *(they are legally foods),* the government does little to regulate their implied *(or explicit by the word of sales clerks)* benefits to the consumer. I wonder. Could the Justice Department, the FTC, or the FDA ever consider their false advertising as sufficient justification for prosecution? Apparently it is easier for these agencies to ignore the billions spent by the easily-duped public then to stop this rampant consumer fraud through law enforcement. I don't suppose that lobbying has played any role in this charade, as well.

Why is it that we are disposed to forcefully restrict those harmless activities that offend some people's moral compass, but are unwilling to deter the every-day, white-collar criminals? Surely we can not believe that false advertising is victimless, or that those who are duped deserve what they get.

In one particularly egregious case of not-really-saying-anything advertising, a company's package wording implies that it prevents colds from airborne contagions. The problem is that implying is not the same as a direct statement, and it can not easily be litigated against as a false writing. Their original packaging entreated us to "*Take at the first sign of a cold symptom or before entering crowded environments"*. This is not exactly a promise for it to accomplish anything, is it? Then in print so small that you may not be able to, or are not interested in reading it, they say *"This product is not intended to diagnose, treat, cure or prevent the common cold"*. So then what is it? Well it's one hell of a money maker, that's what. Then in an attempt to turn their product's liability into an asset, the packaging shouts that it was *"Created by a second grade school teacher"* as if this tidbit of information should be convincing to anyone with more than a second-grade education. Perhaps this female creator had assistance in developing the product from her scriptwriter *(no kidding)* husband.

To date, there is no cure for the common cold and apparently no cure for the common sucker, either.

Again in the not-really-saying-anything department, commercials may start out with a statement talking about how consumers want to save money. One would not be faulted for expecting that the subsequent dialog would have something to do with savings in the following few seconds. But a lack of follow-up information on that particular subject happens far too often, and we are left with a savings-implication that is less than worthless.

If consumers paid critical attention to the multitude of advertising lies, I suspect there would be less of them.

Deceitful Incentives

A product commercial on TV may include the stipulation that it is available for only a limited time. Infomercials invariably express the condition that their offer has a short duration *(just like timeshare salespersons do)*. Oh sure. That's why these same commercials run over and over containing the same time restrictions. They apparently learned this false enticement style from auto salesmen.

This may not apply to every airline mileage card, but it did to ours and probably does to yours. The bankcard's advertising claimed to provide a coach class ticket to anywhere they fly in the US with an accumulation of 25.000 points. No blackouts, no holiday restrictions, virtually all cities. So far, so good, right? Well there is a downside that must be tucked away in the fine print of their contract *(you know, the details that nobody reads)*...

-- if the ticket is for a short hop that an airline carrier may normally charge 15.000 points for, you still pay with 25.000 points

-- tickets are dispensed from the airline's class of least desirable seats with departure times like 6:00am and 6:00pm

-- if an early or late departure is an unacceptable burden, the flyer can pay extra fee *(we experienced $90 up-charge in one case and $150 in another)* per person to receive a more favorable departure time

-- apparently the bank that we <u>had</u> our card with would purchase the cheapest tickets in the marketplace, so our flight from Phoenix to New Orleans went through Atlanta with a long delay... say, isn't Atlanta on the other side of New Orleans from Phoenix?

Then there are the catches incumbent with airline-specific mileage card programs. I attempted to book a flight to Hawaii using points six months in advance of the trip. Initially I was told that those seats were not yet available, the agent didn't know when they would be, and told me to continue checking back. What, every day for six months? On contacting customer service I was told that the 35.000 point seats had been available for 240 days before the flight date and that they had been sold out. However, I could fly for 70.000 points per seat if I wanted... on the same flight and date. The moral of this story is to plan your holiday well in advance to obtain the few seats that are allocated to mileage-points redemption.

Follow-up: In attempting to book two mileage-points flights to New Orleans the following year, I started checking for availability 240 days out as I had previously been instructed. As you might guess, there were no seats available on any flight on or around my preferred departure and return dates, much less at a convenient time of day. After a few days of surfing their web site, a phone call to customer service informed me that those seats are freed up based on a proprietary algorithm *(mathematical formula)* that looks at how fast the plane is filling up. Big demand for seats equals few or no mileage seats. However I could book a 25.000 point flight for 60.000 points each... or more than double the fictional seats. On further checking I discovered first class accommodations to our location were available for 50.000 points each. A no-brainer for me.

Deceitful Banking

If you have been paying attention you may have noticed that there is a proliferation of TV ads for checking-account-connected debit cards. I'm not quite sure why anyone would want one of these cards unless its sole purpose is to limit a child's away-from-home spending to the amount allotted to their account by the parents. Short of that kind of control, I must be missing the point. Don't credit cards work in basically the same way without theses particular limits? Maybe people get debit cards because they have no credit.

A bank's financial justification for the costly promotion of these cards can have only one purpose, and that is to increase its revenues. Ordinarily that might not be a negative scenario, but a portion of the additional revenue is achieved by expecting their cardholders to mistakenly overdraw their bank accounts and incur penalty fees.

Something like one third all purchases are now made with a debit card. Knowing the average consumer's proclivity for misjudging their account balance, bank income must be substantial. In addition, some banks do not permit consumers to opt out of the included overdraft protection plan to eliminate insufficient-balance coverage and penalties. As a result, the cards can be used until denied, regardless of their negative balance. Nice! And of course some of these same practices apply to checking accounts. Overdraft fees can range from $10 to $35 or more if the balance is not brought up to date quickly or is highly overdrawn.

One particularly egregious revenue-generating aspect of the bank's overdraft procedures can be to pay the incoming checks beginning with the largest ones first when there are several presented for processing on the same day. What this does is insure that the client incurs the maximum number of bounced checks. In this scenario a single large check could cause several smaller checks to bounce whereas only one check needed to bounce if the largest were considered last. When questioned about this policy, the bank's rationale was that large checks are probably more important to the customer and should be paid first. You bet.

Note: This practice is now illegal.

Banks should be in business of protecting their client's assets, not to plundering them with high fees and other harmful practices.

Another way the banks bilk the consumer is with changes in the interest rates that they charge. You may qualify for a nominal rate, say around 8-10%, and then have it changed to a much higher rate because you applied elsewhere for an additional credit card or two… perhaps for the sole purpose of receiving a 10% discount on first-day purchases at a department store. So taking advantage of those deals can be very costly indeed. Sometimes it results in the doubling or tripling your previous interest rate for no legitimate reason. The rational *(sure)* may be that receiving additional cards extends your potential debt and is a warning flag *(or is it a target?)* for the banks.

Be aware that <u>potential</u> debt can be assessed as negatively as is <u>actual</u> debt by both the credit reporting agencies and by the banks.

To compound matters, banks appear to be ratcheting down a billing cycle's grace period to twenty-one days… down from what had been the industry standard of twenty-five days. And the banks may be in no big rush to get your statement in the mail. We have seen ours take up to ten days in transit from its closing date. So it's not enough that the credit card companies make a healthy fee on transactions, but they want more, and will think up new ways to get it.

In addition to questionable banking practices, there are the unfair policies of…
-- double cycle billing in which lenders calculate one month's interest fees based on two months of activity the <u>first</u> time that a less than full payment is made
-- allocating customer payments to the charges that have the lowest interest rate *(assuming that the account had been charged different rates at different times, even if the higher rate came first)* and therefore earning more from the higher interest rate

Let us say that you pay off your credit card debt on time each month. Then you inadvertently pay one dollar less than the full amount that is due or are one day late due to mistake or slow mail delivery. The following month you go right back to paying in full. Any reasonably intelligent person would assume that there would be an interest charge for just one month. Wrong. The banks will charge interest two months in a row - potentially doubling your interest rate for that period, and it's all legal. This is patently unfair, but there is no one on your side to stop it.

If you have a $5000 balance at 9% interest rate and then accept a teaser rate of 0% on a $7000 balance transfer *(which converts to 18% in six months)*. Payments will be applied to the $5000 portion of the indebtedness that is being charged the 9% interest. This may sound reasonable at first but the effect is that the interest on the $7000 is coming ever closer, and is at 18%. This becomes an interest landfall for the banks, otherwise why would they offer the teaser?

Note: *In 2010 a law took effect that addressed bank policies. While this went some distance toward fairness, it was hardly circumspect. Even before the regulations became law, the banks were busy inventing new ways to enhance their revenue, such as by increasing interest rates on those who do not have a payment problem. In addition, those who pay their balances off every month may be subjected to an activity fee, or those who do not use their card regularly, to an inactivity fee. I imagine that this is going to be a hit against American Express as cardholders shed those cards that are not universally accepted. There may also be reluctance to waive any first-time overdraft fees or late charges. In 2009 the banks made $39 billion on this service, and it's likely to increase.*

One item that missed the 2010 law is how credit card credits are handled. American Express reduces the balance owed on transactions as soon as the credit has been processed. Visa, on the other hand, does not consider your incoming credits until the next billing cycle. What this means is that you have to initially pay for those items that were returned in one cycle, and then wait to have your statement credited on the next cycle. This is a major windfall for Visa when you consider this huge amount of month to month float as an interest free loan to them.

Because of low inflation and banking overhead, interest rates on CDs are pathetically low, or about a penny on the dollar annually. Unless you have a lot of cash lying around, keeping it in a sock under your mattress is not a bad idea.

The kicker that seems to go with obtaining money from a bank or delivering money to a bank is the omnipresent disclaimer: This offer may be withdrawn at the discretion of the bank at any time. So why is it that a contract allows the bank off the hook at their whim and not the customer? I suggest two possible options for the consumer with these documents. Have the bank remove the offending wording, or go somewhere else.

In 2011 the Federal Reserve was assigned the task of setting the rates *(card swipe fees)* that bankcard processors could charge for their debit and credit transactions. The idea was to have them more closely reflect the cost of processing. Fees typically ran 2-3 percent for credit cards and 1-2 percent for debit cards, and the cost to the consumer *(indirectly)* had grown to $40 billion dollars in 2009.

For years merchants have been complaining that the rates were too high, and forced prices up to cover them. When the Fed proposed limiting bank fees to 12 cents per transaction, the lobbyists got into high gear. One of their claims was that the retailers wanted the consumer rather than themselves to foot the bill. To which I would have to observe that this is what they already do with higher product pricing.

In what may have been posturing, the financial institutions said they might have to stop issuing these cards. Because of the lost income, several banks said they will begin charging debit card holders a monthly fee. So it appears that consumers may not win the fight for fair fees no matter what the feds decided.

In 2012 a consolidate set of suits against the credit card companies shot down the provision that vendors who accept their cards could not charge customers less for paying cash. Now they may do as they please, and we will see how that plays out for consumers. It will be a difficult decision for the vendors because so many people use credit cards, and they may not have an appetite for increased costs.

It turns out that Bankcard companies don't just do the banks bidding. They also play unfairly among themselves. MasterCard and Visa were required in 2008, via settlement of a lawsuit, to pay American Express nearly $4 billion dollars because of their antitrust violations. AmEx had accused a credit card processor of conspiring with MasterCard and Visa to discourage their client banks from issuing Amex cards. This shows how fierce competition for the dollar warps the perspective of big business and encourages the sleaze to come out of the woodwork.

We should note that no individual from Visa, MasterCard, or the processing company was fined or sent to prison. Perhaps AmEx concurred with the court that this is just business, like lines from the Sopranos and other Mafia works.

Bankcard companies also play fast and loose with the credit card's business customers. When they are paid with a credit card, the transaction debits their buye'rs account immediately. But what about paying the seller? They may not get their money until three days later, which amounts to an interest windfall for the bankcard folks. If you tally up how many transactions occur per day and multiply that by an average transaction amount, then total that for the three days that they can invest the vendor's money, interest revenue is significant. And of course it is not shared with the seller who has to wait for his money.

Another way that banks work against people with debt is when they are permitted to manipulate interest rates at their discretion. In the distant past there were usury laws that limited the amount of interest a lender could charge to a borrower to 24%. Now apparently all bets are off because rates in the high 20s and occasionally in the 30's are not uncommon because revolving credit is not considered a loan. Really? Good job lobbyists. And with debt at an all-time high, this has become a big bonus for the lenders. Wouldn't you like to borrow money for a few percent and then lend it out for 25 or 30%? Who needs loan sharks when we have bank sharks?

Banks also use the: *subject to change* disclaimer to alter your credit card contract at will. And of course this is done without your advice and consent because they know that you might not agree.

Going hand in hand with rate obscenity are these contract rules that few of us ever read, until it is too late. For example, if you are late with a car payment, an unrelated credit card company may have the right to double or triple your interest rate on your account with <u>them</u>.

The same might be true if some other credit history that you have is not perfect. Imagine that you have $10.000 of debt on a credit card and inadvertently miss the due-date on some <u>other</u> payment. When this is transmitted to the credit reporting agencies, your credit card company is also privy to that information, and they may invoke their fine print rule #999 where they can arbitrarily increase your interest rate, even though there was no credit offense against their institution. If this happens, the interest burden that you may have been able to manage on the $10.000 debt might now become unmanageable. This is all because the credit bureaus can transmit your information freely *(ok so far)* and the banks can use it as they see fit *(not ok),* and all with virtually no oversight from the government.

Bank Corruption

In 2014 Citigroup, J P Morgan, Chase, Royal Bank of Scotland, HSBC Bank, and USB agreed to a settlement with the various regulating agencies in several countries that totaled just under 3.4 billion dollars. For years these institutions had used their internet communications to manipulate <u>and</u> brag about rigging the currency markets. This regulatory action came on the heels of an investigation of a similar scandal where various financial institutions were involved in illegally fixing the London Inter-bank offered rate or LIBOR.

In addition the US Treasury Department announced that they were fining the largest US banks 950 million dollars for failing to prevent misconduct in their foreign-exchange trading operations. This manipulation of the exchange rates has "a profound effect on the economy" according to the CFTC director. Apparently is was not deemed so profound that a more hefty fine was imposed. $1 billion is chump change to these institutions.

So there are several things that should be apparent here. The banks have demonstrated that they feel that they are above the law, and they were even arrogant enough to brag about their misdeeds on social media sites. Apparently, once again with big business, no one has done jail time for their parts in this banking fraud. While $3.4 billion and $950 million may sound like very large penalties to most of us, they amount to little more than a slap on the wrist for the cash rich banks that were fined. Therefore the fines offer little incentive against future manipulations by those officers and corporations that were involved.

Censorship Express

I have taken the position that censorship, short of not being able to scream *fire* in a theater, is not productive, and it is not for anyone to promote or impose. But there are those who just can't stand to mind their own business.

In 2012 PayPal, the major Internet transaction processor for the credit card companies, dictated to Smashwords *(part of Amazon),* an Internet publisher, that they must remove all of the books from their inventory that deal with incest, bestiality, and rape, or they would be denied PayPal's payment transfer services. This threat carries a lot of weight because of how important their services are to publishers and independent writers. While the credit card processors that are behind the PayPal initiative were not disclosed at this time, it is likely, according to Smashwords, that it was probably all of them.

One has to wonder at why restricting the publishing of legal books would be on the agenda of these companies. How is it that they feel the need to interject themselves into this arena? Aren't there enough pressing problems in this country without big business putting their religious noses into legitimate writings? Censorship is an obscenity that should not be tolerated by any society. And if these businesses were to win this battle, where does their war end. Didn't we learn a lesson from the book burnings in Hitler's Germany?

On the good news front, a few weeks after the fallout from their decision hit the fan, PayPal saw the light *(emails, letters, editorials, phone calls)* and essentially reversed their decision.

On the bad new front, there was a very public book burning of piles of three books in an author's series that included a good deal of very hot sex. One of the males interview over this event complained that the books made it impossible for men to live up to the new expectations, as if these novels became a woman's bibles. My take is… how do meatheads like this ever get their 15 minutes of shame? Oh yea. It's that sex repression thing again.

Back to Banks

The bankers lobbied congress a few years back to dramatically tighten the criteria for exercising bankruptcy that resulted from their own loose credit and debt transfers policies? So have you homesteaded your home in those states which allow it? If not, do it now! This is a consumer protection feature that prevents institutions from attaching a specified amount *(up to 100%)* of the value of your home to service your debt, should you exercise personal bankruptcy. You may have $100.000 or more in home equity dollars that are exempt from credit company seizure. Once the bankruptcy proceeding are over, you could sell your home, recover the equity, and the lenders can not touch it.

Disclaimer… since I am not a lawyer, you are advised to seek appropriate legal council in order to verify my understanding of the law. Ok? And don't you just love it that I have to say this for something so straightforward?

One final indictment against the banking industry. When the financial institutions were consolidating and misrepresenting the risk of their predatory *(insufficient homeowner income)* loan packages, the banks were complicit by selling them forward *(and taking commissions)* to Fanny Mae and Freddy Mac *(FM/FM)*. Then some of them took bail-out money from the feds to stay above water when the housing collapse occurred.

In 2011 the Federal Housing Finance Agency *(FHFA),* with the jurisdiction to oversee FM/FM, sued seventeen major banks which were instrumental in some $200 billion in losses. Their suit alleged that these banks broke state and federal laws with their loan package sales. The FHFA alleged that these home mortgage backed securities *(derivatives)* had been marketed with registration statements and prospectuses that "contained materially false or misleading statements and omission". Regardless of the outcome, my bet is that none of those culpable in this scandal will ever be required to enter into restitution by returning their commissions, or by facing jail time. Wait and see.

Going hand and hand with the housing crisis are the incredible lines in the sand that have been drawn by mortgage banks. Rather than renegotiate their high interest-rate loans, they have mostly chosen to turn out owners who could have managed their debt if the interest rates had been lowered. So instead of promoting good relationships with the communities and maintaining a steady flow of income, these banks saw fit to evict people and shoot themselves in the foot.

In some cases where the homeowners made an effort to negotiate their monthly payments down, bank policies prevented them from even talking about doing a deal unless the homeowners were delinquent in their payments. Yep! Talk about self inflicted wounds.

While there are reasons why the housing crisis occurred, this ongoing foolishness has exacerbated the problem rather than resolve it. And those of us who were not part of this difficulty have seen their home values plummet as well.

Whistleblowers would not be needed in government or business if there were not rampant, corrupt practices going on.

Major corporations would like us to imagine that it is the politicians who are doing *(usually preventing)* the public's bidding, but nothing could be further from the truth. A few of the real power brokers involved in this action are the…
-- financial institutions
-- communications institutions
-- military industrial complex
-- automobile industries
-- health insurance industries
-- pharmaceutical industries
-- agricultural industries
-- oil, gas & coal industries

Executive Embellishment

I suppose for the elite there can be made a case made for excessive executive compensation. They are in the upper echelons of business, and feel that they deserve to be there. In addition, they believe that their contribution to the business far exceeds the small fraction that they receive… i.e. a small piece of a much bigger pie. Maybe you even buy into this self-serving philosophy.

For most of us, our permissiveness with corporate selfishness has led us to circumstances where we sit quietly in the shadows while the business executives make *(not earn)* thousands of times what the government sets as the minimum wage. Lehman Brothers, in one particular case, paid a consultant nearly $1.000.000 <u>per day</u> for 17 days just prior to their receiving $billions in a Fed bailout.

Along the same lines, Goldman Sachs Group, Inc *(GSG)* seems to have become a breeding ground for unrestrained corruption with their all's fair in business attitude… a concept that inexorably flows down from the top of the management ladder. And their deficiencies in fair play are not isolated examples. Executives at the top pay scales have historically shown little regard for their worker's compensation in comparison to their own. The disparity between one's actual worth to a company and their good-ol'-boy network of inflated salaries has been getting more egregious over the years.

In 2013 once again, an activist group has tendered a shareholder proposal to have GSG adopt an independent Board Chairman who has not had affiliations with the bank. GSG's traditional response in these matters has been to ask the SEC to exclude the proposal from its proxy. The subject of chairman independence has become a hot topic among corporation investors these days, but their success rates have been mixed. GSG, with its efforts, has managed to beat back a series of these proposals to date.

Merrill Lynch is reputed to have remodeled its executive's office a while back for an incoming CEO to the tune of $1.2 million. This included chairs for about $15.000 each, a $35.000 toilet, a $1.400 trash can. This is more than the average price of five homes in 2007 dollars. And we haven't touched on his golden parachute, country club membership, chauffeured limousine, executive jet, stock options, and oh yes, base income. Their chauffeur service alone ran some $230.000. Ain't life grand at the top?

In 2012 a portion of the Dodd-Frank package on financial reform, which has been labeled *an internal equity provision*, obligates board members to take into consideration the differential between their executive's pay and the average salary of the company's employees. In recent years, executive pay packages have been rising faster than the inflation index. I guess even the Republicans have had enough of this out of control trend. Of course, looking at an issue is certainly no guarantee that these boards will act to change an outrageous ratio.

Insider Trading Deals

In 2010 Rajat Gupta, a director at GSG, was charged with leaking secrets about the bank's dealings to a hedge fund. One of his insider tips was that Berkshire Hathaway was about to shore up GSG during the financial crisis. In 2012 presiding Judge Rakoff said that this was "disgusting in its implications" and "a terrible breach of trust". So what was the sentence handed down for such a heinous crime? It was two years *(probably to be at some clubhouse jail if the sentence is even upheld)* and a five million dollar fine *(which is chump change to people at this level of banking)*.

Since 2009 six former SAC Capitol Advisors *(founder Steven A Cohen)* employees have been convicted of insider trading. Four are now cooperating with the government, and a seventh was indicted in 2013, thanks in part to information provided by an un-indicted mole. This seventh person, according to a criminal complaint, was involved a conversation with Cohen and followed by the selling of $700 million in holdings of two drug companies. This sale took place just one day before a negative drug-trial announcement was announced. Draw you own conclusion on this.

When criminals rip off the money markets for their own gratification or in some cases for playing the big shot role to their friends, it is not just about the money that <u>they</u> have illicitly made. It is also about the money that <u>others</u> either do not make or actually loose as a result of that action.

Executive Misbehavior

In separate GSG cases with judges, lawmakers, and regulators, it has been suggested that the bank ignored their conflicts of interest and sold investment to its clients that it knew are weak, all in the pursuit of profit. In 2012 in a very public resignation, one of their bankers in London wrote an op-ed article for the New York Times saying that the GSG sells financial products "that they are trying to get rid of". He went on to remark that "It makes me ill how callously people talk about ripping off their clients".

While we are on the subject of ripping off. Morgan Stanley *(MS)* had been sued by the American Civil Liberties Union *(ACLU)* for violating the civil rights laws by encouraging a lender, New Century Mortgage Corp *(NCMC),* to push risky loans in the black neighborhoods of Detroit. The ACLU and others filed the lawsuit on behalf of the homeowners who took out these loans from NCMC. That corporation was a sub-prime lender which has since gone out of business. The lawsuit claims the MS pushed NCMC to make risky loans because MS took a profit at the start of each loan process, and then sold the loans before they could go bad. That left others who were down the derivatives line holding the bag. As you may know, many of these bad loans ended up in Fanny May and Freddie Mac portfolios, which are insured by the federal government (i.e. us).

How Are You Doin'?

Just how much was or will-be your retirement settlement worth? $250.000? Nothing at all? Perhaps you are in the wrong business. The place to be is in large corporation management. Apparently there is a: *you pad my wallet and I'll pad yours* scheme in play at the expense of stockholders and employees. Boards of Directors are aware that the more money they bestow in executive compensation, the more that they are likely to receive for their limited duties. As an example of the limited part, Condoleezza Rice was able to both head up the US State Department and remain on an oil company board at the same time, thereby demonstrating how little work may be required of such figurehead directors. And if she was not devoting sufficient time to her board duties, what do you suspect that she might be getting being paid for by the company? Do I need to spell it out?

There is also a system in place where some executives go from corporate positions, to consultant, to director, to government, to corporate positions, and they benefit from these round-robin journeys because they are very good to others *(reciprocity in action)* in their fraternity. Not to mention, they can collect multiple *(double dip)* paychecks.

These connections may not be a subject that is publicly spoken of, but the players have learned how this corrupt system works. As for the executives, how could there be any other rational explanation for their inflated pay other than reciprocity? Certainly it would not be that they deserve it. So when one in this exclusive club benefits, they all benefit. I am not aware of a board member ever being confronted, dismissed or prosecuted for conflict-of-interest or fiduciary infidelity.

This high level fleecing of companies occurs when stockholders don't make the connection between management rip-offs and their lower dividends and stock prices. Shareholders with very large portfolios may also be part of the problem when they do nothing to correct the situation with their voting rights. This arrangement is somewhat analogous to what happened in the small city in California where the city managers voted themselves and their college's outrageous salaries for doing very little work on the cities behalf. They were, however, busy putting their friends and relatives on the payroll for non-existent jobs.

Another aspect of executive pay revolves around their impressive perks. Personal travel for these people on corporate jets has become commonplace... and not just for the execs, but for the directors that approve this expense as well. A shareholder of Chesapeake Energy Corp. has accused that company of understating the cost of personal travel on their fleet of jets by as much as $10 million per year. The suit alleges that there has been substantial use of this perk, along with the circumvention of public reporting rules. Aircraft expenditures are generally calculated on variable costs such as fuel. They exclude the fixed costs like pilot salaries, maintenance, and the cost of the aircraft. Wouldn't you like to take your next vacation on luxury jet and only pay for your portion of the fuel that is consumed?

The shareholder suit also alleges that the amount of personal travel involves such a "high proportion of the total use" that the fixed costs should be included in their compensation reporting. The fact that variable costs at this company do not count is an outrage to all shareholders. Do we need any more evidence that the company directors and executives have a cozy arrangement when it comes to benefits?

The wealthy make the regulations that benefit the wealthy - Is this coming as a news-flash to you?

How much are we talking about in excessive executive compensation anyway? An example would be the Home Depot's *(HD)* golden parachute to a relatively short term CEO. According to the news reports, after just six years of mediocre performance and much grumbling from the stockholders, he abruptly quit(?). As a result, his severance package was $210.000.000. That's hundreds of millions of dollars folks. Can you imagine what they might have paid him for doing a good job? It is hard to believe that a company even as large as HD would not miss that kind of money. I'm sure the stockholders and lower paid employees would if they could do something about it.

This same executive has taken the helm of another large company, presumably with another extravagant severance package. And that is far from being an isolated example of excess. Packages that are in the hundreds of millions of dollars are more common than you might think. I read about one that was somewhere north of $400.000.000. That is more than $1.000 per day in the average person's lifespan, seven days a week, diapers to diapers.

But not every CEO who is terminated is treated quite so well *(a bit of sarcasm)*. In 2011 Sara Lee Corporation dumped its chief with a pay package valued at only $11.000.000. That is not all that shabby for being fired. If you were let go from your job, you might not even qualify to collect unemployment insurance.

Then there were the unceremonious departures of the CEO's of Fanny Mae and Freddy Mack in 2008 who were also given golden parachutes. Despite their corporations being deeply involved in the packaging *(reselling to investors)* of high risk home mortgage loans,

38

these two received over $30.000.000 in severance pay. That's a nice reward for running their businesses into the ground to the point where they required massive government bailouts.

A survey in 2011 by the Public Affairs Council found that the public had a good opinion of business in general but not of its leadership. And this is even when there are very few people who are intimately aware of the extent of good ol' boy networks and how corrupt the executive compensation is in these exclusive clubs.

Delaware Connection

It turns out that there is a third component in influencing executive pay, and that happens to be the state of Delaware. In return for the revenue that it receives from the incorporations of large businesses, the state's laws and regulations *(according to a statement made by Carl Ichan)* coddle the directors that coddle the executives with their excessive salaries, bonuses and golden parachutes. Delaware also makes it illegal for shareholders to bring a legal action that would move a corporation out of the state. So for their pieces of silver, Delaware allows the unhealthy director-executive connection to function unfettered against the interests of the employees and shareholders. This state qualifies as the same type of venue *(flag)* shopping that is done by foreign shipping companies so that they are not subjected to stricter US rules.

According to a survey, more than 60% of the population believes that the rich are responsible for creating wealth and jobs in this country… apparently ignoring the fact that the middle class has been shrinking for years while the upper class is becoming ever more wealthy. And this percentage of poorly informed, true believers has not deviated significantly in the many decades since the original polling on this subject. So the propaganda that is espoused by the rich has been thoroughly effective. The rest of us just can't seem to get with a rational blame-game to account for people's shrinking income.

Most of us don't even pay due diligence to those billionaires who freely admit that their class is grossly under taxed. In the mean time the sheep are led to the slaughter, and they go along willingly.

Class Warfare

But not everyone goes to the slaughter quite so willingly. In recent years there have been street demonstrations in San Francisco by the people who were being evicted from their rentals and by their supporters. These forced move-outs were initiated in order to make expensive upgrades to accommodate the wallets of the nuevo-riche, like those who may have had their fortunes made in Silicon Valley startups. The hikes in rental prices were driving long time residents out in order for them to find more affordable digs.

The narrator of this particular TV story said something like *'it is ok for the rich to get richer as long as the middle class does not stagnate'*. Well where did this pin head get his economic education and news from? We have tolerated years of shrinking income for the middle class. And where does he think the money for *getting richer* comes from? I don't think they print it. A good deal of it comes from those outrageous tax breaks for the wealthy and from executive income and benefits. The stock options for participants in a new business, if that is the case, come at the expense others who may then own a diluted piece of the company.

Maybe it is about time for class warfare to take hold before there is no middle class with enough clout to make a difference.

Competition Reduction

If a company is limited in the prices it can charge the public due to competition, and is therefore limited in the profits it can make, the solution sometimes lies in eliminating their competition. No, not like what Standard Oil did in the early days of automobiles when it…
-- reduce the price of fuel in locations where there were other gas stations until that competition went out of business
-- then raise their prices where they had eliminated the competition to make up for the losses

Today the answer is to buy out the competition with stock, like smaller Air West's attempt to buy out larger Delta Airlines or US Air's proceedings to buy out American.

Here is one formula. First, make an offer to issue stock to cover the cost of to-be purchased company. One might think that this dilution of a companies stock might serve to distress the investors, but not always. What the buying company and its stockholders receive is the other company and its stock, so the acquiring companies stock is not really watered down. After the purchase occurs, which results in less competition in their field, the acquiring company is in a better position to do things such as…
-- terminate or lay off redundant employees
-- raise prices with less concern because of diminished competition
-- acquire the other company's technology and brain trust
-- reduce worker's health or retirement plans if appropriate
-- increase profits through economies of scale

The consequence for the consumer can be higher prices and reduced innovation. Reduction in business competition is seldom good for the consumer or the economy.

Oversight Reduction

We should be aware that professional groups such as doctors, veterinarians, lawyers, real estate agents, appraisers, etc. are allowed to establish their own oversight committees which function as judge and jury over their members. When a member violates some guideline, sanctions can be applied. So far, so good you say? What you may not be aware of is that these societies are self-governing for the purpose of protecting themselves against government regulations and the public. They can then set up guidelines to limit members of their professions from…
-- being witnesses against each other
-- contradicting each other
-- counseling each another's clients/patients

Because of self-regulation these societies can act as good-ol'-boy networks which then can work against the interests of those who utilize their professional services. It also means that the members can be subject to the whims of the controlling bodies without an appeal through normal civil channels. Can you imagine what the building industry would be like if its contractors were allowed to police themselves? Fortunately they are not a society that can afford lobbyists.

Because the aforementioned groups are generally white collar, organized, and have beau coup money for those lobbyists, they have been granted special privileges from the government that others are not so fortunate to receive. While this is not always a bad thing, it can and does lead to abuse. Without going into detail, when we looked into using a veterinarian oversight committee to sanction a vet for malpractice *(nearly causing the death of a pet)*, we discovered just how uncooperative and protective of their group they can be. The same was true, of course, for the vet's insurance company. So rather than either of these groups protecting the pet owner, they protected the doctor.

White Collar Crime

More on how we under prosecute white collar business persons when they commit non-violent felonies. This is a problem that is not always recognized by the-world-according-to-Republicans who may foolishly believe that businesses are self-regulating.

The numerous complaints that had been made to the Security and Exchange Commission *(SEC)* about the Madoff scam, for example, had fallen repeatedly on deaf ears. And now that this affair has come to light, where are his co-conspirators? Can one man really steal over fifty billion dollars and not have help from dozens of others?

Investment bankers who created the real estate house-of-cards passed on their derivative's risk, eventually to Fanny May, Freddie Mac and others. This con may have been a low-risk/high profit scheme for the bankers, but it created extreme hardships for the millions of homeowners who...
-- shouldn't have been qualified for loans in the first place
-- lost their homes
-- lost equity in their mortgages
-- subsequently damaged the housing market

To date none of these traders has yet to pay back a penny of their ill-gotten commissions, which in some cases ran in the hundreds of millions of dollars. Just let Joe blue collar and try to shoplift a shirt at a department store and stay out of jail. We put our foot down on that kind of behavior.

White Collar Stupid

In 2010, 29 men will killed in the worst US coal mining disaster in decades at the Upper Big Branch mine in West Virginia. In 2011 a jury found the security chief guilty of lying to the investigators who were probing that explosion. He was also found guilty of the disposal of thousands of security-related documents at the Massey Energy Company mine. So rather than being a help with the investigation, he earned a date with a sentencing hearing.

In 2010 the Gulf of Mexico experienced the world's worst oil spill. It substantially exceeded that of the Exxon Valdez in 1989 which ran aground *(thanks to an inattentive captain)*. BP, the owners of the drilling rig that failed, has been rightly accused of several *well-duhs* when they…
-- drilled far below the 18.000 foot depth that was permitted
-- had not installed the blowout prevention device that should have been located 200 feet in the seabed *(they reportedly saved about $50.000 by skipping this device)*
-- installed only one switch that could stop the oil flow, and that may have been located where the explosion occurred, leaving the remaining crew with no options
-- tried to encourage the fishermen who were voluntarily helping in the containment to sign waivers of liability against BP should something go wrong
-- made an effort to lay the blame for the spill on the company that operated the rig
-- claimed that their liability was limited, after endlessly repeating that they would take full responsibility for the spill

Thanks to Vice President Chaney's assurance years earlier *(you may recall that he and President Bush came from the oil industry)*, the oil companies were guaranteed that their blowout liability would be limited to $75 million… an incredibly tiny amount when compared to the Gulf of Mexico's cleanup price tag that ran into the billions of dollars, or compared to BP's $5.6 billion profit for the quarter in which the spill occurred.

It should come as no surprise to anyone that major companies would play fast and loose with their liability. Corporate America's first responses to misdeeds are denial and subterfuge. It does not much matter that it was BP which was the responsible party in this particular case. Other large corporation might have pursued the same course of action.

Business integrity revolves around the bottom line for the executives and shareholders *(which include the executives)*. On top of this tragedy you have the deep-thinker Rush Limbaugh taking sides with BP. I wonder if that was because he is also big business and empathizes with others in that class.

By mid 2011 only a few billion of the $20 billion cleanup fund had been allocate to those who suffered damages. On the other hand, the law office of Kenneth Fienberg was receiving $15 million per year to oversee BP's disbursements while the victims struggled to receive any or full compensation in time to save their businesses. I would have done Fienberg's job for a whole lot less. All along, BP was repeatedly feeding us the propaganda that they were doing all that they could to help those in need.

On the surface it seems like Fienberg's concerns for the little guys also appears to be minimal. Or perhaps it is just one more situation where big business gets special breaks from those who are part of or sympathetic to big business.

In 2012 BP began a major ad campaign telling us how well the clean-up and recovery of businesses the Gulf States was taking place. No real examples, just blather. And the press seemed to be in no great hurry to dispute the claims. So in the subsequent years we should believe that everything is getting back to normal. Sure.

Undeserved Credit

It has taken years to overcome the technological problems and business reluctance required to begin producing a low sulfur diesel fuel. As frequently happens, Europe is ahead of us in the areas of conservation and pollution control because they do not permit the oil companies to dictate policies to them... as least not as much as we do. They are concerned with the environmental impact of excessive use of fuels.

But as soon as the mandated European-style reformulation of the fuel for cars sold in Europe was completed in the US, the oil industry creatives were prepared with their self-promoting ads that took credit for this achievement. There is just no hint of integrity with the oil companies because their oligopoly status insures that there can be a lack of veracity and responsibility to the consumer.

Deserved Discredit

While most of us believe that there is sufficient evidence to support the CO2 connection to global warming, there is a minority that is still intent on debunking that theory about the cause of the current warming trend. Among them is a major oil company which has for years funded a company-line think tank dealing with this subject. In their efforts to distract the public from the peril, they offered a fee to any author that could make *(make-up?)* a case against the idea that global warming is man-made.

The industry's attempt to deter the public from the notion of our planet being in environmental jeopardy is similar to the tobacco industries campaign in the 1980's of trying to convince us that their products were not hazardous to our health. You may remember that each tobacco CEO swore under oath before Congress that they were unaware of any credible connection to cancer and other health concerns. This level of deceit is now being practiced by big oil with their employing several of the tobacco industries techniques, such as...
-- funneling money to sympathetic Congresspersons who have no integrity *(I guess that covers just about all of them)*
-- engaging in disingenuous and attention diverting advertising
-- providing financial support for disinformation articles and speakers that pretend to be unbiased
-- sowing doubt wherever possible

The problem with consumers is that their apathy toward self education lends them to being easily manipulated. Listening to what experts say rather than paying attention to conscienceless promoters and politicians is not high on peoples wave length.

Invasion of Privacy

Many Americans take for granted that we have the legal protection against the invasion of personal privacy. They might be surprised to learn that the Constitution offers no such specific assurances. Yes, the framers did include a Bill of Rights with related provisions in this area. Among them are...
-- privacy of beliefs *(1st Amendment)*
-- privacy of a home against demands that it be used to house soldiers *(3rd Amendment)*
-- privacy of a person and possessions against unreasonable searches *(4th Amendment)*
-- privacy of personally held information... aka the privilege against self-incrimination *(5th Amendment)*

As for this last amendment, we may mistakenly construe that our personal information has been protected by the force of law. Nothing could be further from the truth. While no one can compel us to reveal our secrets *(except by granting immunity or in some cases, the threat of contempt)*, this is exactly what we do voluntarily on a routine basis.

Public revelations can come about when our personal transactions take place in the public domain, such as through banking, borrowing, purchasing, using the courts, and the Internet. And nearly all of this data is recorded by companies who make our information their own business in order to sell that data to interested parties, including the government.

These data capturing companies maintain records on virtually all of us, and their databases include the billions of transaction that take place and are recorded in the public domain. It is collected, collated, and served up to the buyers who may glean, among other things, what are our...
-- home address and phone numbers
-- religious preferences

-- buying habits
-- mortgage debt
-- family structure
-- court history
-- individual and family income
-- offenses that we may have committed

Ever since George Orwell's classic book dealing with the perils of big brother government there have been the occasional, dire warnings from a handful of citizens as to the adverse consequences of having power concentrated in the hands of a few. For years we have been warned of this encroachment into our private lives, and the warnings have gone mostly unheeded.

Sure, there are a number of fringe groups that extol the evils of the state, but they too are largely ignored. That is unless they address their grievances with violent or illegal action. With their paranoia comes the imagined repression which serves to fuel their extremist beliefs. Need I mention the initials NRA as a dedicated group loosely falling into this mindset?

Who would have thought that it would be businesses and Internet criminals, rather than our government, who are leading the assault on our being left to live in peace and quiet? Forget for the moment the malicious hackers who inflict harm for their monetary advantage. Business spam and click-tracking on the Internet are pervasive, and it is trending ever more in that direction. When you browse on the net there is software that wants to know what you are buying and what your surfing habits are in order to target you for future invasions.

When I joined the Air Force many years ago I was surprised to learn that they were aware of a traffic ticket that I had received. Now if this information could be so easily obtained by some entity before mass computerization, what do you think today's snooping capabilities are?

A big-brother exposé revealed that Google has kept a record of every inquiry ever made by every person who has ever used their search engine. While they claim that they have no nefarious motive for this failure to delete, they are not spending millions of dollars on data storage for nothing. It is only a matter of time before they decide to sell this data to those companies who will use it to pigeonhole our activities for whatever motives they might have. And the folks at Google had the brass to lobby *(successfully)* to have their company excluded from a privacy protection law.

In 2011 MasterCard and Visa announced their intentions to tie their vast databases of credit card purchases to each cardholder's online experiences for the purpose of targeted advertising. These product connections would then be sold to companies so that they could provide ads that may reflect our interests. For example, if you subscribed to an automobile magazine, you might be subjected to receiving car ads on your browser. While the details of this new form of database mining had not been worked out as of this writing, the handwriting is on the wall.

Back in 2011 Fair Isaac *(the folks who brought us the FICO credit scoring)* announced that they are branching out into the new area *(for them)* that involves the understanding of human behaviors. This is not an intellectual quest, but rather it is being done to determine the ways to predict our actions in order to sell that information to those companies which will use it to their own advantage.

I suppose there are some who will not consider these probes into our lives to be much of an invasion of privacy. Perhaps they can even be viewed as being an improvement on the annoying, pointless ads we are now inundated with. Count me out on that score.

Invasion By Software

When I receive an offer to upgrade an installed piece of freeware I wonder how much of the new coding is devoted to improving the product and how much of it is directed at nagware *(those popup solicitations to upgrade to a pro version, or worse).* One piece of anti-malware had reverted to issuing several-times-daily nags about upgrading, in contrast to their previous monthly or the-computer-has-been-rebooted schedule.

Another piece of freeware *(Ad-Aware)* repeatedly tried to install a toolbar even after I un-clicked the box to permit it. When this toolbar popup failed to go away I uninstalled the software. When that did not get rid of the nagware, another piece of software that I use came on the screen telling me how to rid the computer of this persisting annoyance. Fortunately my computer background allowed me to understand and follow their technical instructions and clear the last remnants of the software. I imagine that other, less trained users just go nuts.

With some helpware software, the cure can be worse than the original problem.

If one is not circumspect about paying close attention to each new version during its installation, it may download an unwanted toolbar, change your browser's home page, change your browser, or add other pieces of software that are either unwanted or unsafe.

More than once I have had to uninstall offending software to rid my computer from attached nuisanceware. Sometime the software is embedded so deeply into the computer's innards that highly specialized products are required to get the job done. Fortunately for me, I have thirty plus years of dealing with computer ills to fall back on. My sympathies to those who don't. Still, once in every few years or so I have to completely flush the computer, reinstall the operating system, and then reinstall all of my software to get back to normal... a very time consuming process.

After updating one freeware product I immediately began receiving junk mail that continued in spite of reporting it to a government site. Trying to unsubscribe to these senders of garbage only serves to guarantee that you will receive even more junk mail in the future because you have now verified your email address to the bad guys. This well-intended but pointless action may result in having your address sold to other bad guys.

If you are receiving a lot of junk email and your browser has an auto-block option, that feature can be useful feature. If not, your best option may be to abandon the old address and create a new one. Hopefully your contact list is up to date so that you can notify one and all about the change.

I received a series of no subject emails from a neighbor, which I immediately deleted. Later he sent out a warning message to those in his address book that he had been hacked. My reply to him *(as politely as I could)* was that this problem occurred due to some action he had taken, and that he may want to hone in on the cause so as to not have it happen again. It is less likely that his situation came about because of someone else's poor computer judgment, a stolen email list is one for example, but that is always possible.

As I have advocated forever, never click on any links at unknown web sites or on links of any kind sent to you by friends. The chances of infecting your computer with this action are substantial. The only exception to this rule might be an attachment that you know was created by the sender… such as photos. But even then you can never be positive of the contents without contacting the sender in advance of opening.

Those of us who buy books at traditional shops do expect anonymity from those interests who may want to profile us. But this is turning out not to be the case with the increasingly popular downloaded ebooks. The purveyors have our email addresses and selection tastes to use as they see fit because the government has yet to protect us with any meaningful extension to privacy laws.

Now it is unlikely in the extreme that information about the sales of these ebooks will be used in a seriously nefarious way. However, it will certainly contribute to the flood of spam that reaches inboxes or with the ads that pop up on browsers. Then it is only a matter of time before the data is marketed to others for their own purposes, just like our public records now are. Computers have the capacity to store and collate zillions of pieces of information, and they are being used for that exact purpose.

Of course we have all read-about/heard-about the profusion of identify theft cases. By now we should all know about shredding our documents rather than just trashing them. In spite of this there are millions who want every detail of their lives broadcast over the social networks. Undoubtedly this is because of the mild brain high that I mentioned earlier. But no good act goes unpunished. The bad guys have taken to extracting and using this inside information to impersonate the blather-er to their elderly relatives, using horror stories about their needing emergency money. Then they asked to have the money sent ASAP before the story can be verified.

Kip's Books & Links

The books listed here are available in ebook format for Kindle™ and Nook™ readers at Amazon.com and elsewhere. Some of the shorter materials are "ideas" booklets or excerpts from longer books. Hard copy books are available at Createspace.com. The URL links, where listed, access book previews.

A BETTER BATHROOM - An Ideas Guide
Construction
https://www.createspace.com/Preview/1134187
$1.99   34 pages

A BETTER KITCHEN - An Ideas Guide
Construction
https://www.createspace.com/Preview/1134190
$1.99   36 pages

AGGRESSION & BULLYING - It's Not Just Our Wiring
Human Nature
$1.49   11 pages

AN OUTDOOR KITCHEN - The Latest Trend?
Construction
$1.49   6 pages

BEFORE STARTING HOME CONSTRUCTION - What You Need To Know In Advance
Construction
https://www.createspace.com/Preview/4136208
$2.99/$5.49   40 pages

BRAIN CHOICES & FREE WILL - Getting To Know Ourselves Using Concepts That Are Not Well Understood Or Accepted
Human Nature
https://www.createspace.com/Preview/1134191
$3.99/$5.99   78 pages

CUSTOM HOME DOs & DON'Ts - The ULTIMATE Guide To Getting Your Custom Home DONE RIGHT!
Construction
https://www.createspace.com/Preview/1134192
$6.99/10.49   266 pages

DECEPTION IN AMERICA - How We Are Manipulated Big Business, Politicians, The Press & Our Indoctrinations

Government/Business/Politics
https://www.createspace.com/Preview/1134195
$9.99/15.99   458 pages

EVOLUTION, THE BRAIN, & RELIGION - How Evolution Made Us What We Are
Human Nature
https://www.createspace.com/Preview/1134196
$4.99/$6.99   160 pages

EXCESSIVE EXECUTIVE COMPENSATION - What You Should Know About
The Fleecing Of America By Executives & Boards
Government/Business/Politics
$1.49   11 pages

FOLLOWING THE CROWD - How We Fall In Line With Others
Human Nature
$1.49   14 pages

FUN WITH APPETIZERS - For Those Who Like To Entertain Well
Cookbook
https://www.createspace.com/Preview/4438108
$3.99/$5.99   70 pages

FUN WITH CARBOS - The Cookbook For Those Without A Care
Cookbook
https://www.createspace.com/Preview/4440041
$3.99/$5.99   94 pages

FUN WITH CHICKEN - The Fowl & Seafood Cookbook That Avoids Red Meat
Cookbook
https://www.createspace.com/Preview/4441007
$4.99/$6.99   148 pages

FUN WITH DESSERTS - The - What To Do When The
Meal Is Over - Cookbook
Cookbook
https://www.createspace.com/Preview/4444531
$2.99/$5,49   64 pages

FUN WITH ENTREES - Getting To The Heart Of Cooking
Cookbook
https://www.createspace.com/Preview/1135491
$5.99/$8.99   172 pages

FUN WITH MEAT - The Carnivore's Cookbook
Cookbook

https://www.createspace.com/Preview/4436803
$3.99/$5.99   110 pages

FUN WITH SALADS - My Take On The Classics & Others
https://www.createspace.com/Preview/1136150
$1.99/$5.49   24 pages

FUN WITH SEAFOOD – See Food & Eat It Cookbook
Cookbook
https://www.createspace.com/Preview/4494327
$3.99/$5.99   84 pages

FUN WITH SOUP - It's Economical, & Healthy As Well
Cookbook
https://www.createspace.com/Preview/4442511
$1.99/$5.49   38 pages

FUN WITH WINE - Aging And Tasting Wine
$1.49   9 pages
An informative guide, including wine-term explanations.

GOVERNMENT FOR PEOPLE? - How the US government "functions" without regard for the negative ramifications of its actions
Government/Business/Politics
https://www.createspace.com/Preview/1134204
$3.99/$5.99   88 pages

HOME DESIGN GOALS - Important Considerations
Construction
https://www.createspace.com/Preview/1134209
$1.99/$5.49   36 pages

HOME GREEN HOME - The Ins & Outs Of Home Efficiency
Construction
https://www.createspace.com/Preview/1134208
$2.99/$5.49   42 pages

HOW BUSINESS FAILS US - What You Need To Know About Business Corruption
Government/Business/Politics
https://www.createspace.com/Preview/1134206
$2.99/$5.49   70 pages

HOW WE LEARN, WHY WE DON'T - Getting To Know Ourselves
https://www.createspace.com/Preview/1134212
$3.99/$5.99   86 pages

INCONVENIENT REALITY - How Big Business Shoots Us In The Foot, & How Congress And The Press Helped Get Us Into This Mess
https://www.createspace.com/Preview/1134213
Government/Business/Politics
$5.99/$8.99   190 pages

INVADING YOUR PRIVACY - What You Don't Know And What You Should Know
Government/Business/Politics
$1.49   18 pages

LAW IS FOR LAWYERS - The People That We Rely On For Our Protection Can Be The Biggest Offenders Of It
Government/Business/Politics
$1.99   22 pages

ONE POT CLASSICS - The Comfort Food & Easy Clean-up Cookbook
Cookbook
https://www.createspace.com/Preview/1134289
$6.99/$11.49   306 pages

PATHETIC POLITICS & PERFORMANCE - What We Should Know About Our System Of Government
Government/Business/Politics
https://www.createspace.com/Preview/1134290
$4.99/6.99   112 pages

POWER BREEDS ABUSE - Or To Put This Another Way... On Some Level, Power Always Leads To Corruption
Government/Business/Politics
https://www.createspace.com/Preview/1134291
$2.99/4.99   48pages

SELECTING A CONTRACTOR - Making The Right Choice The First Time
Construction
$1.49   11 pages

SELLING & STAGING A HOME - Getting The Most From Your Efforts
Construction
$1.49   6 pages

SENIOR FRIENDLY HOME DESIGN - Making A House Safe
Construction
$1.49   11 pages

SOCIAL NETWORKING - The Downside To Exposing Yourself
Human Nature
$1.49   5 pages

THE PRESS'S ROLE IN BAD POLITICS - What They Do, And How They
Contribute
Government/Business/Politics
https://www.createspace.com/Preview/1134295
$1.99/$5.49   32 pages

THE WAR ON DRUGS - How It Harms Everyone
Government/Business/Politics
$1.49   6 pages

TO SELL OR REMODEL - Making The Right Decision
Construction
$1.99   9 pages

TRAVEL DEALS & BARGINS – Gaming The System To Win
Travel
$1.49   14pages

www.ingramcontent.com/pod-product-compliance
Lightning Source LLC
Chambersburg PA
CBHW030734180526
45157CB00008BA/3160